Christmas Around the W[

By Mary P. Pringle

History Project

Table of Contents

As early as two thousand years before Christ Yule-tide was celebrated by the Aryans. They were sun worshipers and believed the sun was born each morning, rode across the upper world, and sank into his grave at night.

Day after day, as the sun's power diminished, these primitive people feared that he would eventually be overcome by darkness and forced to remain in the underworld.

When, therefore, after many months, he apparently wheeled about and grew stronger and stronger, they felt that he had been born again. So it came about that at Hweolor-tid, "the turning-time," there was great rejoicing at the annual re-birth of the sun.

In the myths and legends of these, our Indo-European ancestors, we find the origin of many of the Yule-tide customs now in vogue.

According to the Younger Edda, Wodin or Odin, the pioneer of the North, a descendant of Saturn, fled out of Asia. Going through Russia to Saxland (Germany), he conquered that country and left one of his sons as ruler. Then he visited Frankland, Jutland, Sweden, and Norway and established each one of his many sons on a throne.

This pioneer traveler figures under nearly two hundred different names, and so it is difficult to follow him in his wanderings. As Wodin, he established throughout the northern nations many of the observances and customs common to the people of the Northland today.

The Edda gives an ancient account of Balder, the sun-god, who was slain because of the jealousy of Loki (fire). Loki knew that everything in nature except the mistletoe had promised not to injure the great god Balder. So he searched for the mistletoe until he found it growing on an oak-tree "on the eastern slope of Valhalla." He cut it off and returned to the place where the gods were amusing themselves by using Balder as a target, hurling stones and darts, and trying to strike him with their battle-axes. But all these weapons were harmless. Then Loki, giving the twig of mistletoe to the blind god, Hoder, directed his hand and induced him to throw it. When the mistletoe struck Balder it pierced him through and through and he fell lifeless.

So on the floor lay Balder dead; and round
Lay thickly strewn swords, axes, darts, and spears,
Which all the Gods in sport had idly thrown
At Balder, whom no weapon pierced or clove;
But in his breast stood- fixt the fatal hough

Of mistletoe, which Lok the Accuser gave
To Hoder, and unwitting Hoder threw —
'Gainst that alone had Balder's life no charm.

Great excitement prevailed among the assembled gods and goddesses when Balder was struck dead and sank into Hell, and they would have slain the god of darkness had it not occurred during their peace-stead, which was never to be desecrated by deeds of violence. The season was supposed to be one of peace on earth and goodwill to man. This is generally attributed to the injunction of the angels who sang at the birth of Christ, but according to a much older story the idea of peace and good-will at Yule-tide was taught centuries before Christ.

According to the Edda, gifts from the gods and goddesses were laid on Balder's bier and he, in turn, sent gifts back from the realm of darkness into which he had fallen. However, it probably is from the Roman Saturnalia that the free exchange of presents and the spirit of revelry have been derived.

The Druids held the mistletoe in great reverence because of its mysterious birth. When the first new growth was discovered it was gathered by the white-robed priests, who cut it from the main bough with a golden sickle never used for any other purpose.

The food peculiar to this season of rejoicing has retained many features of the feasting recorded among the earlier people. The boar made his appearance in mythological circles when one was offered as a gift to Frey, god of rain, sunshine, and the fruits of the earth. This boar was a remarkable animal; he could run faster than a horse, through the air and over water. Darkness could not overtake him, for he was symbolical of the sun, his golden bristles typifying the sun's rays.

At one time the boar was believed to be emblematical of golden grain, as he was the first to teach mankind the art of plowing. Because of this service he was most revered by our mythological ancestors.

In an account of a feast given in Valhalla to the dead heroes of many battles, Saehrimnir, a sacred boar, was served. Huge pieces were apportioned to the deceased heroes and the meat had such a revivifying affect that, restored to life, they called for arms and began to fight their battles over again.

An abundance of heavenly mead made from goats' milk and honey was provided for the feasts and on occasion ale, too, was served.

Toasts were usually drunk in honor of Bragi, god of poetry, eloquence, and song. The gods pledged themselves to perform remarkable deeds of courage and valor as they tossed off horn after horn of mead and ale. Each time their mighty valor grew until there was no limit set to their attainments. It is possible that their boastful pledges may have given rise to the term, to brag.

Apples were the favorite fruit, as they prevented the approach of age and kept the gods and goddesses perpetually young and vigorous.

Certainly Yule-tide was a very merry season among the ancient people who feasted, drank, and danced in honor of the return of the sun, the god of light and new life.

When messengers went through the various countries bearing tidings of a new religion and of the birth of a Son who brought light and new life into the whole world, they endeavored to retain as many of the established customs as possible, but gave to the old-time festivals a finer character and significance.

As the fact of Christ's birth was not recorded and there was no certainty as to its date, the early Christian Fathers very wisely ascribed it to Yule-tide, changing the occasion from the birthday of the sun to that of the Son. For a while the birth of Christ was celebrated on dates varying from the first to the sixth of January; on the dates of certain religious festivals such as the Jewish Passover or the Feast of Tabernacles; but the twenty-fifth of December, the birthday of the sun, was ever the favorite date.

Pope Julius, who reigned from 337 to 352 A. D., after a careful investigation, considered it settled beyond doubt that Christ was born on or about the twenty-fifth of December, and by the end of the fifth century that date was very generally accepted by Christians. The transition from the old to the new significance of Yule-tide was brought about so quietly and naturally that it made no great impression on the mind of the masses, so nothing authentic can be learned of the early observance of Christmas.

The holly, laurel, mistletoe, and other greens used by the Druids still served as decorations of the season, not as a shelter for fairies, as in former days, but as emblems of resurrection and of immortal hope.

The glorious luminary of day, whether known as Balder, Baal, Sol, or any other of the innumerable names by which it was called by the primitive peoples, still gladdens the hearts of mortals at Yuletide by "turning-back" as of old; only today it yields its place to a Superior Power, in whose honor Yule-tide is observed.

All Christendom owes a debt of gratitude to its pagan forbears for the pleasant features of many of its holidays and especially for those of Yule-tide. The Fathers of the early church showed rare wisdom in retaining the customs of these ante-Christian festivals, imbuing them .

with the spirit of the new faith and making them emblematic of a purer love and hope.

New Year's Day as a feast day is one of the oldest, if not the oldest, on record. It is mentioned by Tacitus in the First Century, but first referred to as a Christian festival about the year 567.

In Rome the day was dedicated by Numa to the honor of god Janus, for whom Julius Caesar named the month of January. Numa ordained that it should be observed as a day of good-humor and good fellowship. All grudges and hard feelings were to be forgotten. Sacrifices of cake, wine, and incense were to be made to the two-faced god who looked forward and backward. Men of letters, mechanics, and others were expected to give to the god the best they had to offer of their respective arts. It was the great occasion of the entire year, as it is now in many countries.

The date of New Year's Day has varied among different nations. Among the Egyptians, Chinese, Jews, and Romans it has been observed on dates varying from March first to December twenty-fifth. It was as late as the Sixteenth Century before the date of January first was universally accepted as the New Year by the Romans. Nations retaining the Gregorian calendar, such as Russia and Greece, observe it thirteen days later than those who reckon time by the Julian calendar.

Among northern nations the love of fire and light originated the custom of kindling bonfires to burn out the old year and destroy all evil connected with its past. Light has long been an expression of joy and gladness among all branches of the Aryan race.

The Greek and Latin Churches still term Christmas the "Feast of Lights," and make it a period of brilliancy in Church and home. The Protestant covers the Christmas tree with lighted candles and builds a glowing fire on the hearth. The innate love of light and warmth—the inheritance from the sun-worshipers of ages past—is always dominant in humanity at Yule-tide festivals.

No country has entered more heartily into Yule-tide observance than England. From the earliest known date her people have celebrated this festival with great ceremony. In the time of the Celts it was principally a religious observance, but this big, broad-shouldered race added mirth to it, too. They came to the festivities in robes made from the skins of brindled cows, and wearing their long hair flowing and entwined with holly.

The Druids in the temples kept the consecrated fires burning briskly. All household fires were extinguished, and anyone wishing to rekindle the flame at any time during the twelve days preceding Yule-tide must buy the consecrated fire. The Druids also had a rather unique custom of sending their young men around with Yule-tide greetings and branches of mistletoe. Each family receiving this gift was expected in return to contribute generously to the temples.

With the coming of the Saxons, higher revelry reigned, and a Saxon observance of Yule-tide must have been a jolly sight to see. In the center of the hall upon the open hearth blazed a huge fire with its column of smoke pouring out through an opening in the thatched roof, or, if beaten by the wind, wandering among the beams above. The usually large family belonging to the house gathered in this big living-room. The table stretched along one side of the room, and up and down its great length the guests were seated in couples. Between them was a half-biscuit of bread to serve as a plate. Later on this would be thrown into the alms-basket for distribution among the poor.

Soon the servers entered carrying long iron spits on which they brought pieces of the meats, fish, and fowls that had been roasted in iron pans suspended from tripods out in the yard.

Fingers were used instead of forks to handle the food, and the half-biscuit plates received the grease and juices and protected the handsome bord-cloth.

There was an abundance of food, for the Saxons were great eaters. Besides flesh, fish, and fowls their gardens furnished plenty of beans and other vegetables, and their ort-geards produced raspberries, strawberries, plums, sweet and sour apples, and cod-apples, or quinces. The cider and stronger drinks were quaffed from quaint round-bottomed tumblers which, as they could not stand up, had to be emptied at a draught.

The Saxons dined at about eleven o'clock and, as business was not pressing in those days, could well afford to spend hours at the feast, eating, drinking, and making merry.

After every one had eaten, games were played, and these games are the same as our children play today—handed down to us from the Old Saxon times.

When night came and the windows no longer admitted the light of the sun, long candlesticks dipped in wax were lighted and fastened into sockets along the sides of the hall. Then the makers, or bards as they came to be called in later days, sang of the gods and goddesses or of marvelous deeds done by the men of old. Out-of-doors huge bonfires burned in honor of Mother-Night, and to her, also, peace offerings of Yule cakes were made.

It was the Saxon who gave to the heal-all of the Celts the pretty name of mistletoe, or mistletan,—meaning a shoot or tine of a tree. There was jollity beneath the mistletoe then as now, only then everybody believed in its magic powers. It was the sovereign remedy for all diseases, but it seems to have lost its curative power, for the scientific men of the present time fail to find that it possesses any medical qualities.

Later on, when the good King Alfred was on the English throne, there were greater comforts and luxuries among the Saxons. Descendants of the settlers had built halls for their families near the original homesteads, and the wall that formerly surrounded the home of the settler was extended to accommodate the new homes until there was a town within the enclosure. Yule within these homes was celebrated with great pomp. The walls of the hall were hung with rich tapestries, the food was served on gold and silver plates, and the tumblers, though sometimes of wood or horn, were often of gold and silver, too.

In these days the family dressed more lavishly. Men wore long, flowing ringlets and forked beards. Their tunics of woolen, leather, linen, or silk, reached to the knees and were fastened at the waist by a girdle. Usually a short cloak was worn over the tunic. They bedecked themselves with all the jewelry they could wear; bracelets, chains, rings, brooches, head-bands, and other ornaments of gold and precious stones.

Women wore their best tunics made either of woolen woven in many colors or of silk embroidered in golden flowers. Their "abundant tresses," curled by means of hot irons, were confined by the richest head-rails. The more fashionable wore cuffs and bracelets, earrings and necklaces, and painted their cheeks a more than hectic flush.

In the Fifteenth and Sixteenth Centuries the magnificence of the Yule-tide observance may be said to have reached its height. In the old baronial halls where:

The fire, with well-dried logs supplied,

Went roaring up the chimney wide,

Christmas was kept with great jollity.

It was considered unlucky to have the holly brought into the house before Christmas Eve, so throughout the week merry parties of young people were out in the woods gathering green boughs, and on Christmas Eve, with jest and song, they came in laden with branches to decorate the hall.

Later on, men rolled in the huge Yule-log, emblematic of warmth and light. It was of oak if possible, the oak being "sacred to Thor, and was rolled into place amidst song and merriment.

Each member of the family, seated in turn upon the log, saluted it, hoping to receive good luck. It was considered unlucky to consume the entire log during Yule; if good luck was to attend that household during the coming twelve months, a piece ought to be left over with which to start the next year's fire.

The boar's head held the principal place of honor at the dinner. So during September and October, when the boar's flesh was at its best, hunters with well-trained packs of boar-hounds set out to track this savage animal. They attacked the boar with spears, or surrounded him and drove him into nets. He was a ferocious antagonist to both dogs and men, and when sore pressed would wheel about, prepared to fight to the death. Before the dogs could grip him by the ear, his one weak point, and pin him down, his sharp teeth would often wound or even kill both the hunter and his dogs. The pluckier the animal the louder the praise sung in his honor when his head was brought into the hall.

The great head, properly soused, was borne in on an immense salver by the "old blue-coated serving-man" on Christmas day. He was preceded by the trumpeters and followed by the mummers, and thus in state the boar's head was ushered in and assigned to its place on the table. The father of the family or head of the household laid his hand on the dish containing the "boar of atonement," as it was at one time called, swearing to be faithful to his family and to fulfill all his obligations as a man of honor. This solemn act was performed before the carving by every man present. The carver had to be a man of undaunted courage and untarnished reputation.

Next in honor at the feast was the peacock. It was sometimes served as a pie with its head protruding from one side of the crust and its wide-spread tail from the other; more often the bird was skinned, stuffed with herbs and sweet spices, roasted, and then put into its skin again, when with head erect and tail outspread it was borne into the hall by a lady—as was singularly appropriate—and given the second place on the table,

The feudal system gave scope for much magnificence at Yule-tide. At a time when several thousand retainers were fed daily at a single castle or on a baron's estate, preparations for the Yule feast—the great feast of the year—were necessarily on a large scale, and the quantity of food reported to have been prepared on such occasions is perfectly appalling to Twentieth-Century feasters.

In 1248 King Henry III held a feast in Westminster Hall for the poor which lasted a week. Four years later he entertained one thousand knights, peers, and other nobles, who came to attend the marriage of Princess Margaret with Alexander, King of the Scots. He was generously assisted by the Archbishop of York who gave £2700, besides six hundred fat oxen. A truly royal Christmas present whether extorted or given of free will!

More than a century later Richard II held Christmas at Litchfield; two thousand oxen and two hundred tons of wine were consumed. This monarch was accustomed to providing for a large family, as he kept two thousand cooks to prepare the food for the ten thousand persons who dined every day at his expense.

Henry VIII, not to be outdone by his predecessors, kept one Yule-tide at which the cost of the cloth of gold that was used alone amounted to £600. Tents were erected within the spacious hall from which came the knights to joust in tournament; beautiful artificial gardens were arranged out of which came the fantastically dressed dancers. The Morris (Moresque) Dance came into vogue in England during the reign of Henry VII, and long continued to be a favorite. The dancers were decorated from crown to toe in gay ribbon streamers, and cut all manner of antics for the amusement of the guests. This dance held the place at Yule that the Fool's Dance formerly held during the Roman Saturnalia.

Henry VII's daughter, Elizabeth, kept the season in great magnificence at Hampton Court where plays written for the occasion were presented.

This feature of Yule observance, which is usually attributed to Rowena, daughter of Vortigern, dates back to the grace-cup of the Greeks and Romans which is also the supposed source of the bumper. According to good authority the bumper came from the grace-cup which Roman Catholics drank to the Pope, au bon Pere. The wassail bowl of spiced ale has continued in favor ever since the Princess Rowena bade her father's guests Wassheil.

The offering of gifts at Yule has been observed since offerings were first made to the god Frey for a fruitful year. In olden times one of the favorite gifts received from tenants was an orange stuck with cloves which the master was to hang in his wine vessels to improve the flavor of the wine and prevent its molding.

As lords received gifts from their tenants, so it was the custom for kings to receive gifts from their nobles. Elizabeth received a goodly share of her wardrobe as gifts from her courtiers, and if the quality or quantity was not satisfactory, the givers were unceremoniously informed of the fact. In 1561 she received at Yule a present of a pair of black silk stockings knit by one of her maids, and never after would she wear those made of cloth. Underclothing of all kinds, sleeves richly embroidered and bejeweled, in fact everything she needed to wear, were given to her and she was completely fitted out at this season.

In 1846 Sir Henry Cole is said to have originated the idea of sending Christmas cards to friends. They were the size of small visiting-cards, often bearing a small colored design—a spray of holly, a flower, or a bit of mistletoe—and the compliments of the day. Joseph Crandall was the first publisher. Only about one thousand were sold the first year, but by 1862 the custom of sending one of these pretty cards in an envelope or with gifts to friends became general and has now spread to other countries.

During the Reformation the custom of observing Christmas was looked upon as sacrilegious. It savored of popery, and in the narrowness of the light then dawning the festival was abolished except in the Anglican and Lutheran Churches. Tenants and neighbors no longer gathered in the hall on Christmas morning to partake freely of the ale, blackjacks, cheese, toast, sugar, and nutmeg. If they sang at all, it was one of the pious hymns considered suitable—and sufficiently doleful—for the occasion. One wonders if the young men ever longed for the sport they used to have on Christmas morning when they seized any cook who had neglected to boil the hackin and running her round the market-place at full speed attempted to shame her of her laziness.

Protestants were protesting against the observance of the day; Puritans were working toward its abolishment; and finally, on December 24, 1652, Parliament ordered "That no observance shall be had of the five and twentieth day of December, commonly called Christmas day; nor any solemnity used or exercised in churches upon that day in respect thereof."

Then Christmas became a day of work and no cheer. The love of fun which must find vent was expended at New Year, when the celebration was similar to that formerly observed at Christmas. But people were obliged to bid farewell to the Christmas Prince who used to rule over Christmas festivities at Whitehall, and whose short reign was always one of rare pleasure and splendor. He and other rulers of pastimes were dethroned and banished from the kingdom. Yule cakes, which the feasters used to cut in slices, toast, and soak in spicy ale, were not to be eaten—or certainly not on Christmas. It was not even allowable for the pretty Yule candles to be lighted.

Christmas has never regained its former prestige in England. Year after year it has been more observed in churches and families, but not in the wild, boisterous, hearty style of olden times. Throughout Great Britain Yule-tide is now a time of family reunions and social gatherings. Ireland, Scotland, Wales, and the Islands each retain a few of their own peculiar customs, but they are not observed to any extent. In Ireland—or at least in some parts—they still indulge in drinking what is known as Lamb's-wool, which is made by bruising roasted apples and mixing the juice with ale or milk. This drink, together with apples and nuts, is considered indispensable on Christmas Eve.

England of all countries has probably known the merriest of Yule-tides, certainly the merriest during those centuries when the mummers of yore bade to each and all

A merry Christmas and a happy New Year,
Your pockets full of money and your cellar full of beer.

There seems always to have been more or less anxiety felt regarding New Year's Day in England, for "If the morning be red and dusky it denotes a year of robberies and strife."

If the grass grows in Janivear
It grows the worse for't all the year.

      And then very much depended upon the import of the chapter to which one opened the Bible on this morning. If the first visitor chanced to be a female, ill luck was sure to follow, although why it should is not explained.

      It was very desirable to obtain the "cream of the year" from the nearest spring, and maidens sat up till after midnight to obtain the first pitcher full of water, supposed to possess remarkable virtues. Modern plumbing and city water-pipes have done away with the observance of the "cream of the year," although the custom still prevails of sitting up to see the Old Year out and the New Year in.

      There was also keen anxiety felt as to how the wind blew on New Year's Eve, for

If New Year's Eve night wind blow South,
It betokeneth warmth and growth;
If West, much milk, and fish in the sea;
If North, much cold and storm there will be;
If East, the trees will bear much fruit;
If Northeast, flee it man and brute.

Yule-tide in Germany

It was away back in the time of Alexander the Great that Germany was made known to the civilized world by an adventurous sailor named Pytheas, a man of more than ordinary talent, who was sailing northward and discovered a land inhabited by a then unknown people. He reported his discovery to the Romans, but the difficulty was that Pytheas had seen so much more than any of the Greeks or Romans of those days that they utterly refused to believe his statements. Time has proved that the sailor was nearer right in many of his apparently visionary statements than his countrymen dreamed, although it has taken centuries to prove the fact in some cases.

The people whom Pytheas then introduced to the polite world were Teutons, a branch of the great Aryan race and closely related to the early English. The men were simple, truthful, and brave, but were sadly addicted to drink, it was said, and consequently were often quarrelsome. The women were much like those of today in their characteristics: virtuous, proud, and dignified; very beautiful, with golden-hued hair, blue eyes, and fresh, fair complexions. Like most of the early peoples, the Teutons worshiped gods and goddesses, and so have many customs and traditions in common with other branches of the Aryans.

If England has enjoyed the merriest Yule-tides of the past, certainly Germany enjoys the merriest of the present, for in no other country is the day so fully and heartily observed. It is the great occasion of the year and means much to the people.

For a week or more before the day, loads of evergreen trees of all sizes may be seen coming into the cities and towns to be piled up in squares and open places until the entire place looks like a forest of small firs. One wonders where they all come from and for how many years the supply will last, but it is not likely to fail at present.

The Lutherans gave Martin Luther the credit of introducing the Christmas tree into Germany. He may have helped to make it popular, but certainly there is abundant evidence to prove that it was known long before the Reformer's time. It is generally supposed to have its origin in mythological times and to be a vestige of the marvelous tree, Yggdrasil.

Possibly Martin Luther thought of the old story of the tree and imagined, as he traveled alone one cold night, how pretty the snow-laden fir trees along his path would look could they be lighted by the twinkling stars overhead. But whether he had anything to do with it or not, the tree is now one of the most important features of Yule-tide among the Germans of all denominations.

Nearly ten million households require one or two trees each Christmas, varying in height from two to twenty feet. Societies provide them for people who are too poor to buy them, and very few are overlooked at this happy holiday season.

The grand Yule-tide festival is opened on the eve of St. Nicholas Day, December sixth; in fact bazaars are held from the first of the month, which is really one prolonged season of merrymaking.

In Germany, St. Nicholas has a day set apart in his honor. He was born in Palara, a city of Lycia, and but very little is known of his life except that he was made Bishop of Myra and died in the year 343. It was once the custom to send a man around to personate St. Nicholas on St. Nicholas Eve, and to inquire how the children had behaved through the year, who were deserving of gifts, and who needed a touch of the birch rods that he carried with him into every home. St. Nicholas still goes about in some parts of the country, and in the bazaars and shops are sold little bunches of rods, real or made of candy, such as St. Nicholas is supposed to deal in. In some places Knight Rupert takes the place of St. Nicholas in visiting the houses. But Kriss Kringle has nearly usurped the place St. Nicholas once held in awe and respect by German children.

Because St. Nicholas Day came so near to Christmas, in some countries the Saint became associated with that celebration although in Germany the eve of his birthday continues to be observed. Germans purchase liberally of the toys and confectionery offered at the bazaars, and nowhere are prettier toys and confectionery found than in Germany—the country which furnishes the most beautiful toys in the world.

From the palace to the hut, Yule-tide is a season of peace, rest, joy, and devotion. For three days, that is the day before Christmas, Christmas, and the day after—known as Boxing-day—all business not absolutely necessary to the welfare of the community is suspended. Stores, markets, and bazaars present a festive appearance; the young girl attendants are smiling and happy, and everyone seems in the best of humor.

Many of the poorer class of Germans do not eat much meat, but at Christmas all indulge in that extravagance, so the markets are unusually crowded. They all like to purchase a plant or a flower for Christmas and the flower stores are marvels of beauty and sweetness.

Everyone is busy preparing for the great occasion. Grown folks become children again in the simplicity of their enjoyment and enter into the excitement with as much enthusiasm as do the children.

Newspapers are not generally published during the three days of business suspension, for no one would have time or interest to read them at such a season.

In many places churches are open during the week before Christmas, for with all the bustle and excitement incident to the preparations, the people, young and old, are filled with a deep spirit of devotion, and never for an instant forget the significance of the occasion they commemorate.

Churches are not trimmed nor are they made attractive with flowers, songs, or in any special way, but the people go to listen with devotion to the telling of the old, old story of Christ's birthday and of the first Holy Night at Bethlehem.

The day before Christmas all are busy trimming up their homes and preparing for the great day. Usually the mother of the household trims the tree, not admitting any other member of the curious and expectant family into the room. Tables are provided for holding the gifts, as everyone in the family is expected to make a gift to every other member, and it is surprising to note the interest taken in these simple gifts—often a soap-rose, an artificial flower, knitted lace, even sausages, cheese, or butter—and with each and all the ever-present Christmas cake. It is spiced and hard, out into every manner of device—men, women, animals, stars, hearts, etc. The pepper cakes or some similar cakes are to be seen everywhere at Christmas time.

The gifts are often accompanied with short verses, good, bad, or indifferent, according to the talent of the giver, but all serve to make the occasion merry. In some families these simple inexpensive gifts are so carefully kept that collections may be seen of gifts received by different members of the family since their infancy.

On Christmas Eve the guests assemble early, and by six o'clock a signal is given for the door of the mysterious room to be opened to admit the family to the tree:

0 Hemlock-tree! 0 Hemlock-tree! How faithful are thy branches
Green not alone in summer time,
But in the winter's frost and rime
O Hemlock-tree! Hemlock-tree! How faithful are thy branches

It is ablaze with tiny lighted tapers and radiant with shiny tinsel cut in pretty devices or in thread-like strips. Bright balls, gay toys, and paper flowers help to enhance its beauty, and sometimes scenes from sacred history are arranged with toys at the base of the tree.

With the distribution of the gifts the fun begins; each person is expected to kiss every other person present and help make the occasion a merry one.

Holy Night, or as the Germans term it, Weihnacht—the Night of Dedication—is the time of family reunions, fun, and frolic. Not alone in homes, hospitals, prisons, barracks, and elsewhere is the pretty be-tinseled tree to be seen on Christmas, but in burying-grounds, on the resting-places of the dead, stand these fresh green trees in evidence of keeping the loved one's memory green.

While the custom of having a tree is universal throughout Germany, and from thence has been introduced into other countries, there are many customs peculiar to certain sections. In some of the little out-of-the-way places in the Tyrolese Alps the old-time Miracle Plays are enacted in a most primitive manner. As the peasants rarely, if ever, attend the theatre or have any opportunity to see a modern play, this occasion attracts them from far and near. Where is the theatre, who are the actors, do you ask? The theatre is the largest place available, sometimes a large room, sometimes a barn, anything that will accommodate the crowd that is sure to come. In one description of a play given on Christmas Day it is stated that the people assembled in a barn belonging to the vicarage to witness the Paradise Play. The top of a huge pottery stove at least five feet high served for the throne of God the Father, the stove being hidden by screens painted to represent clouds. The play "began at the beginning,"—at Chaos. A large paper screen bedecked with a profusion of suns, moons, stars, and comets formed a background, while in front sprawled a number of boys in tights with board wings fastened to their shoulders to represent angels. The language was as simple and primitive as the scenery, yet for the credulous, devout peasants "no distance is too great, no passes too steep or rough, no march on dusty highroads too fatiguing, if a Miracle or Passion Play is their goal."

Does it seem sacrilegious? Not to those who attend it in the spirit of humility and devotion, as do these Tyrolese peasants. In some places plays are given in churches on Christmas as they were formerly in England, but these are not common, and are only found in remote places. Throughout this country there is always a church service in the morning which is very generally attended, Protestants and Catholics alike making Christmas the day of all the year in which they attend church.

The name Christmas probably originated from the order that was given for saying mass (called Christ-mass) for the sins of the people on the day that commemorates the Savior's Birth.

One beautiful feature of a German Christmas is the widespread thought for the poor and the interest taken in them. Many wealthy families have charge of a certain number of poor families, and on Christmas Day invite them to their own luxurious homes to receive gifts and enjoy the tree prepared for them. An address, prayer, and song as they stand around the tree precedes the distribution of gifts, usually of clothing and food, with which the guests fill the bags and baskets they bring with them. And for all there is an abundance of pepper cakes, or some other Christmas cake.

In the midst of all the excitement of lighted tree and pretty gifts, German children seldom forget to return thanks for what they receive. They are taught that all these gifts come through the Christ-child, and that the occasion is not for selfish enjoyment but to give pleasure to others, and that no one is too poor to give kindly thought and pleasant words to those around them.

In some parts of Germany—Lorraine is one—the people burn the Yule-log; sometimes a huge log that will last through the three days' festivity, sometimes one so small that the family sit before it until it is all consumed. Sometimes a part of the log is suspended from the ceiling of the room and each person present blows at it hoping to make a spark fall on some watching face; then again some carry a piece of the log to bed with them to protect them from lightning. But the Yule-log is not very generally known in this land of great pottery stoves and closed fireplaces, and that may be one reason why post-wagons go rumbling about at Christmas time, carrying parcels from place to place and from door to door, blowing their post-horns continuously, instead of the parcels being dropped down chimneys by Santa Claus.

It is customary, also, in some parts of the country, for the people and their animals to fast the day before Christmas. At midnight the people attend church and it is said that the cattle kneel; then both man and beast partake of a hearty meal. There are places in the German Alps where it is believed that the cattle are blessed with the gift of language for a while on Christmas Eve, but as it is a very great sin to listen, no one has yet reported any conversation among them. In another part of the country it is thought that the Virgin Mary with a company of angels passes over the land on Holy Night, and so tables are spread with the best the larders afford and candles are lighted and left burning that the angelic visitors may find abundant food should they chance to stop on their way.

Boxing-day, when boxes prepared for the poor are distributed, follows the Holy Day and after that business is resumed, although festivities do not cease.

Sylvester, or New Year's Eve, is the next occasion to be observed during Yule-tide. The former name was given in honor of the first pope of that name, and still retained by many. After the usual church service in the early evening, the intervening hours before midnight are spent in the most boisterous merriment. Fun of all sorts within the limit of law and decency prevails. Any one venturing forth wearing a silk hat is in danger of having his hat, if not his head, smashed. "Hat off," cries the one who spies one of these head-coverings, and if the order is not instantly obeyed, woe betide the luckless wearer. At midnight all Germany, or at least all in the cities and the larger towns, may be seen out-of-doors or leaning from windows, waiting for the bells to ring out the Old Year and welcome in the New. At first stroke of the bells there arises one universal salute of Prosit Neujahr (Happy New Year).

It is all good-natured fun, a wild, exuberant farewell to the Old Year—the closing scene of the joyous Yule-tide.

Yule-tide in Scandinavia

"TO Norroway, to Norroway," the most northern limit of Scandinavia, one turns for the first observance of Christmas in Scandinavia, for the keeping of Yule-tide in the land of Odin, of the Vikings, Sagas, midnight sun, and the gorgeous Aurora Borealis. This one of the twin countries stretching far to the north with habitations within nineteen degrees of the North Pole, and the several countries which formed ancient Scandinavia, are one in spirit regarding Christmas although not in many other respects.

In the far north among the vast tribe of Lapps, in their cold, benighted country, as Christmas approaches each wandering tribe heads its reindeer toward the nearest settlement containing a church, that it may listen to the story of the first Christmas morn which is told year after year by the pastor, and yet is ever new and interesting to the people who come from great distances, drawn over the fields of crisp snow by their fleet-footed reindeer.

The Lapp is apparently a joyless individual. Men, women, and children seem bereft of all power of amusement beyond what tends to keep them alive, such as fishing, hunting, and traveling about to feed their herds of reindeer. They have no games, no gift for music, they never dance nor play cards, but year after year drag out an existence, living within low earth-covered huts or in tents. Even the best homes are low and poorly ventilated. For windows are not needed where darkness reigns for months together, where the sun is not seen at all during six or seven weeks of the year, and where people live out-of-doors during the long summer day of sunlight that follows.

In their low, stuffy homes which at Christmas are filled with guests from the wandering Lapps, there is no room for the pretty tree and decorative evergreens. The joy afforded these people at Yule-tide is in the reunion of friends, in attending church services, in the uniting of couples in marriage, and, alas, in the abundance of liquor freely distributed during this season. The children are made happy by being able to attend school, for at Christmas they are brought into the settlements with friends for this purpose. They have only a few weeks' schooling during the year, from Christmas to Easter, and while the schoolmasters are stationed at the little towns, the children work hard to gain the knowledge of books and religion which they crave.

In this terrible winter night of existence, amidst an appalling darkness of Nature and Mind, the one great occasion of the year is Christmas. Not the merry, bright, festive occasion of their more favored brothers and sisters, but what to them is the happiest in the year.

Christmas Eve passes unnoticed. The aurora may be even more beautiful than usual, its waving draperies more fantastic, more gorgeous-hued, but it is unnoticed by the Lapps who have seen it from childhood. Men, women, children, servants, guests, and animals, crowd into the small, low homes, without a thought of Santa Claus coming to visit them. Children have no stockings to hang up, and there are no chimneys for Santa to descend. In fact, he and his reindeer, with their loads of treasured gifts, probably left this region with the sun, bound for more congenial places.

The church bells break the terrible silence of the sunless towns on Christmas morning, and as the fur-encased natives wend their way to church, greeting one another as they meet, there is a faint approach to joyousness. Of course there must be real sorrow and joy wherever there is life and love, although among the Lapps it is hard to discern.

During Yule-tide the Lapps visit one another, attend to what governmental business there may be, give in marriage, christen the children, and bury the dead, whose bodies have lain beneath their covering of snow awaiting this annual visit of the Norwegian clergyman for their final interment.

Think of Christmas without a tree, without wreaths and flowers, without stockings full of gifts, with a dinner of reindeer meat and no plum pudding! And imagine what would be his sensation could a Lapp child be put into a home in England, America, Germany, or even in other parts of Scandinavia what would he say could he receive such gifts as were given you last Christmas!

But Lapps are only a small part of the population of Norway. Norwegian children have many jolly times around the Christmas trees and enjoy hunting for their little gifts which are often tucked away in various places for them to find. Then there are all sorts of pretty games for them to play and quantities of appetizing food prepared for their pleasure. The young folks earn their feast, for all day long before Christmas they are busy tying bunches of oats and corn on the trees, the fences, the tops of houses and of barns, and on high poles which they erect in the yards, until

> *From gable, barn and stable*
> *Protrudes the birdies' table*
> *Spread with a sheaf of corn.*

The Norwegians begin their Christmas with divine services, after which they meet together for a repast which is an appetizer for the feast to follow. A pipe of tobacco is given to each man and boy present, then they smoke while the feast, the great feature of the day, is being made ready. Fish, poultry, meats, and every variety of food known to the Norwegian housewife is served in courses, between which toasts are given, health drunk, and the songs of Norway rendered. Among the latter "Old Norway" is always included, for the people never forget the past history of their beloved country.

One of the pretty customs of these occasions is that each guest on arising turns to the host and hostess, who remain seated at either end of the table, and, bowing to each, expresses his thanks for the meal.

Sometimes after the serving of tea at seven o'clock, little boys in white mantles, with star-shaped lanterns and dolls to represent the Virgin and the Holy Babe, enter the room and sing sweet carols. Often strolling musicians arrive, such as go from place to place at Christmas. After a large supper the guests depart on sledges for their homes, which are often miles distant.

Do you suppose on Christmas Eve, as they look toward the fading light in the West, the children of Norway ever think of their Scandinavian cousins, the little Icelanders, in their peat houses, on that isolated island in the sea, where the shortest day is four hours long, and where at Christmas time the sun does not rise above the horizon for a week, and wonder how they are celebrating Yule-tide?

Christmas is a great day with them also, for they cling to the old songs and customs, and could the west wind convey the sound of glad voices across the wide expanse of water separating the island from the mainland, Norwegian children might hear the Icelandic children singing one of their sweet old songs.

In Sweden there is a general housecleaning before Christmas; everything must be polished, scrubbed, beaten, and made clean, and all rubbish burned, for dirt, like sinful thoughts, cannot be tolerated during the holy festival.

As early as the first of December each housewife starts her preparations for the great day. Many have worked all the year making gifts for the occasion, but now the carpets must come up and be beaten, the paint must be cleaned, and the house set in order. The silver which has been handed down from generation to generation, together with that received on holidays and birthdays, has to be cleaned and polished, so must the brasses —the tall fire-dogs, the stately andirons, and the great kettles—all must be made to reflect every changing ray of light.

Then the baking for a well-ordered household is a matter of great moment, and requires ample time. It is usual to begin at least two weeks before Christmas. Bread is made of wheat and rye flour, raised over night, then rolled very thin and cut into discs twelve or fourteen inches in diameter, with a hole in the center. After having been baked, these are strung on a stick and left to dry under the beams of the baking-room. As they will keep a long while, large quantities are made at this season in each household.

Then follows the making of sweetened, soft, rye, wheat, and other breads, as well as the baking of the light yellow (saffron), the chocolate-brown, and thin gray-colored cakes, and those that are filled with custard.

The preparing of Christmas drinks always requires the close attention of good dames, for there must be an inexhaustible supply of Christmas beer, made of malt, water, molasses, and yeast, and wine with almonds and spices, and various other decoctions.

Then the cheese must be made ready, not only the usual sour kind, but the more delicious sweet cheese that is made of sweet milk boiled slowly for hours and prettily molded.

The Swedish wife is relieved of the burden of making pies, as her people know nothing about that indigestible mixture so acceptable to American palates.

The festivities begin with the dressing of the tree the day before Christmas. In this the older members of the family, with friends and relatives, join with great gusto, preparing paper flowers with which to bedeck the tall evergreen tree which reaches from floor to ceiling.

They cut long ribbons of colored paper for streamers, and make yards of paper fringe to wind with the tinsel among the boughs, from which are hung bright colored boxes of sweetmeats, fruit, and fancy balls.

The children are, of course, excluded from the room and obliged to content themselves with repeating the tales of Santa Claus, as told by their elders. When a gift is offered in person, or, as is more generally the case, is thrown in the door suddenly by an unseen hand, there rings a merry Glad Frill (Good Yule) meaning "Merry Christmas," for that is the wish of the preceding day or days, rather than of Christmas itself.

On Christmas Eve at early nightfall, when the colored candles are ablaze over the entire tree, and the great red ball of light shines from its topmost branches, the children are admitted to the room amidst a babel of shouts and screams of delight, which are increased upon the arrival of a veritable Santa Claus bestrewn with wool-snow and laden with baskets of gifts. On the huge sled are one or more baskets according to the -number of bundles to be distributed in the family. Each bundle bears the name of the owner on its wrapper, together with funny rhymes and mottoes, which are read aloud for the amusement of all. Santa Claus always gives an abundance of valuable counsel and advice to the young folks as he bestows upon them his pretty gifts.

After the distribution of gifts and the disappearance of Santa Claus, all join in dancing and singing around the tree simple, childish jingles such as the following:

"Now is Christmas here again,
Now is Christmas here again,
After Christmas then comes Easter,
Cheese and bread and Christmas beer, Fish and rice and Christmas cheer
—etc."

One of the prettiest dances is that of "Cutting the Oats," in which girls and boys—there must be an extra boy—dance in a circle, singing:

Cut the oats, cut the oats,
Who is going to bind them I
That my dearest will have to do,
But where will I find him

I saw him last eve in the moonlight,
In the moonlight clear and bright,
So you take one and I'll take one,
And he will be left without one.

The boys represent the cutters and the girls the oats, and great merriment prevails as the cutters' arms encircle the waists of the pretty oats, leaving the unfortunate cutter, whom they all dance around, bowing scoffing as they shout:

No one did want you,
Poor sprite, no one wants you,
You are left alone,
You are left alone.

Many of their games are similar to *Blind Man's Buff, Hunt the Key*, and *Hot and Cold*, or *Hunt to the Music*, the latter being one which by its modulations from pianissimo to forte indicate the hunters' nearness to the object sought for. The game of *Blind Feeding the Blind* causes much amusement among the juveniles; two players sit opposite each other blindfolded and endeavor to feed one another with a spoon full of milk, and their mishaps are very entertaining to the on-lookers.

Between the hours of ten and eleven comes the grand Christmas supper, when all adjourn to the dining-room to partake of the annual feast for which the housewives have long been preparing. The table is usually tastefully and often elaborately trimmed with flowers and green leaves. The corners of the long snow-white homespun cloth are caught up into rosettes surrounded with long calla or other leaves; possibly the entire edge of the table is bedecked with leaves and flowers. The butter is molded into a huge yellow rose resting on bright green leaves, and the napkins assume marvelous forms under the deft fingers of the artistic housewives.

The Christmas mush holds the first place in importance among the choice viands of the occasion; it is rice boiled a long while in milk and seasoned with salt, cinnamon, and sugar, and is eaten with cream. Several blanched almonds are boiled in the mush and it is confidently believed that whoever finds the first almond will be the first to be married. While eating the mush, each one is expected to make rhymes about the rice and the good luck it is to bring them, and the most remarkable poetical effusions are in order on these occasions.

The Christmas fish is to the Swede what the Christmas roast-beef is to the Englishman, an indispensable adjunct of the festival. The fish used resembles a cod; it is buried for days in wood ashes or else it is soaked in soda water, then boiled and served with milk gravy. Bread, cheese, and a few vegetables follow, together with a pudding made of salt herrings, skinned, boned, and cut in thin slices, which are laid in a dish with slices of cold boiled potatoes and hard-boiled eggs, covered with a dressing of cream, butter, and eggs—then baked and served hot.

The fish, rice, and a fat goose are said to be served at every table on Christmas from that of the king to that of the commonest of his subjects.

Christmas morning opens with an early service in church, to which the older members of the family go in sled parties of from forty to fifty sleds, each drawn by one, two, or even three horses, over whose backs jingle rows of silver-toned bells. The sled parties are an especial feature of Christmas time. They start out while the stars are still twinkling in the sky, and the lighted trees are illuminating the homes they pass.

The day itself is observed with less hilarity than other days during the season; the "Second Christmas," or day following, being far gayer. Then begin the family parties, with the looking forward to the great Twelfth-Night ball, after which the children and young folks end their evening parties by un-trimming the tree of their entertainer amidst peals of laughter, songs, and shouts.

The tree, of course, has been supplied anew with candles, fruit, and candy. The first are blown out and the last two struggled for while the tree is drawn slowly toward the door out of which it is finally pitched by the merry crowd.

The Swedes have four legal holidays at Yule, beginning the day previous to Christmas, and they make merry while they last. Besides having the Jul-gran or Christmas tree, each family places in the yard a pole with a sheaf of grain on top for the birds' Christmas dinner, a pretty custom common to many countries.

Business is very generally suspended during Christmas, the day following, Twelfth Day, and the twentieth day.

"Do as your forefathers have done, and you can't do wrong," is said to be the motto of the Swedes. So the customs of their forefathers are strictly observed at Yule-tide.

Svea, the feminine name of Sweden, the "Queen of the North," contains what is popularly believed to be the burial-places of Wodin, Thor, and Freya. The mounds are about one mile from Upsala and are visited by travelers from all parts of the world. Antiquarian researchers, however, have recently had a word to say in doubt whether these mounds contain the remains of the renowned beings, those ancient travelers. The Swedes, however, still cling to the belief that the bones of Wodin, the Alexander of the North, rest beneath the sod at Upsala. In these mounds have been found the bones of a woman and of a dog, a bracelet of filigree work, and a curious pin shaped like a bird, but no sign of Wodin's presence. Yet peasants believe that Wodin passes by on dark nights, and his horse's shoe, with eight nail-holes, is exhibited in the museum at Utwagustorp.

New Year's Day is of comparatively little importance; the Christmas trees are usually relighted for the enjoyment of the poorer children and gifts are made to the needy. The Yule festivities are prolonged for two weeks in many places, during which the people visit from home to home and enjoy many social pleasures. The devout attend church services each day, abandon all work so far as possible, and on January thirteenth generally finish up the joyous season with a ball.

The Swedes do not trim their churches with evergreen at Yule-tide as that is an emblem of mourning with them, and is used instead of crape on the door and often strewn before the hearse and also upon the floor in the saddened homes, so of course at Christmas they would not think of using it for decorations. But where they can afford it or can procure them, they use flowers to decorate their homes.

In Denmark, Christmas is a time of unusual merriment and rejoicing. No one who can possibly avoid it works at all from the day before Christmas until after New Year, but spends the time in visiting, eating, and drinking. "May God bless your Christmas; may it last till Easter," is the usual salutation of the season.

With the people of Denmark the favorite dish for Christmas dinner is a goose; everyone, even the cattle, the dog, and the birds, receive the best the larder affords on this occasion. There is a peculiar kind of cake that is made for each member of every family, and, for some reason not explained, the saltcellar remains on the table throughout Yule-tide.

Those who own fruit-trees feel it incumbent upon them to go at midnight on Christmas Eve and with a stick in hand strike each tree three times saying as they do so, "Rejoice, 0 Tree,—rejoice and be fruitful."

In Denmark it is believed by many that the cattle rise on their knees at midnight on Christmas Eve, but no one ever seems to have proved this saying to be true.

In this country also the children delight in listening to stories of trolls who have been driven to the island of Born-hem by the parsons although they once ran riot through Zealand, and the little folks sing pretty songs of Balder, the sun god, which are a special feature of the season.

It is customary to usher in the New Year with a noise of firearms of every description.

Yule-tide in Russia

In this enormous kingdom which covers one-sixth of the land surface of the globe, and where upwards of fifteen million human beings celebrate in various ways the great winter festival of Yuletide, it will be found that the people retain many traditions of the sun-worshipers, which shows that the season was once observed in honor of the renewal of the sun's power. With them, however, the sun was supposed to be a female, who, when the days began to lengthen, entered her sledge, adorned in her best robes and gorgeous head-dress, and speeded her horses summerward.

Russian myths indicate a connection with the Aryans in the remote past; their songs of the wheel, the log, the pig or boar, all show a common origin in centuries long gone by.

Russia to most minds is a country of cold, darkness, oppression, and suffering, and this is true to an altogether lamentable extent. But it is also a country of warmth, brightness, freedom, and happiness. In fact, there are so many phases of life among its vast population that descriptions of Russian life result about as satisfactorily as did those of Saxe's "Three blind men of Hindustan," who went to see the elephant. Each traveler describes the part he sees, just as each blind man described the part he felt, and each believes he knows the whole.

There are certain general features of the Yule-tide observance that are typical of the country. One is the singing of their ancient Kolyada songs, composed centuries ago by writers who are unknown. They may have been sacrificial songs in heathen days, but are now sung with fervor and devotion at Christmas time.

In some places a maiden dressed in white and drawn on a sledge from house to house represents the goddess of the Sun, while her retinue of maidens sing the Kolyada, or carols. Here again appears the ancient custom of gift-making, for the maidens who attend the goddess expect to receive gifts in appreciation of their songs.

The word Kolyada is of doubtful origin. It may refer to the sun, a wheel, or a sacrifice; there is no telling how, when, or where it originated, but the singing of these songs has been a custom of the people from time immemorial, and after the introduction of Christianity it became a part of the Christmas festivities.

Strangely enough the Russians make the Moon the master of the mansion above, and the Sun the mistress, a twist about in the conception of these luminaries worthy of the Chinese, and possibly derived from some of Russia's Eastern invaders. In the above song, the Stars, like dutiful children, all wish their luminous parents good health,

For many years, for many years.

In parts of Russia, the Virgin Mary and birds take the place of the Sun and Stars in these songs, which are sung throughout the Yule season by groups of young folks at social gatherings, or from house to house, and form the leading feature of the Christmas festivities.

It is hard to realize that the stolid, fur-clad Russian is a child of song, for such seem to belong to sunny climes, but throughout his life from the cradle to the grave he is accompanied with song. Not modern compositions, for they are quite inferior as a rule, but those melodies composed ages ago and sung repeatedly through generation after generation, usually accompanied with dancing in circles.

The Kolyadki cover a variety of themes relating to the gods, goddesses, and other celestial beings; to all of whom Christian characteristics have been given until they now form the sacred songs of Yule-tide.

On Christmas Eve it is customary for the people to fast until after the first service in church. They pray before their respective icons, or sacred pictures, recite psalms, and then all start for the church, where the service is, in most respects, the same as in the Roman Catholic Church. There are many denominations besides the established church of the country that hold services on Christmas Eve; but to whichever one goes, it is wise to hasten home and to get to bed in season to have a pleasant Christmas Eve dream, as such is sure to come true, according to Russian authority.

On Welikikdenj—Christmas—the people partake of an early meal. In some parts of the country it is customary to send extremely formal invitations in the name of the host to the guests who are expected to arrive that day. These are delivered by a special messenger and read somewhat as follows:

"My master and mistress beg you to consider, Father Artanon Triphonowitsch, and you, Mother Agaphia Nelidowna, that for thousands of years it has been thus; with us it has not commenced, with us it will not end. Do not, therefore, disturb the festival; do not bring the good people to despair. Without you there will be no pleasure at Philimon Spicidonowitsch's, without you there will be no maiden festival at Anna Karpowna's."

Who could absent himself after such an invitation as this? The place of meeting has been decided upon weeks earlier, for it must be with a well-to-do family possessing a large home to accommodate the guests that usually assemble at Christmas. The "fair maidens," each with her mother and retinue, arrive first on the scene, bringing cake and sweetmeats and gifts for the servants. They would sooner freeze in their sledges before the gate than be guilty of alighting without first receiving the greeting of their host and hostess. Having been welcomed, they next pray before the icon, and then are ready for the pleasures arranged for them.

One peculiar phase of these house-parties is the selecting of partners for the maidens, which is done by the hostess, the "elected" sometimes proving satisfactory and sometimes not. They feast, play games, go snowballing, and guess riddles, always having a jolly good time. Reciters of buiinas (poems) are often present to sing and recite the whole night through, for of song and poetry the Russian never tires.

A pretty custom very generally observed is the blessing of the house and household. The priest visits each home in his district, accompanied by boys bearing a vessel of holy water; the priest sprinkles each room with the water, each person present kissing the cross he carries and receiving his benediction as he proceeds from room to room. Thus each home is sanctified for the ensuing year.

The familiar greeting of "Merry Christmas" is not heard in Russia unless among foreigners, the usual salutation on this day being "Greetings for the Lord's birth," to which the one addressed replies, "God be with you."

The observance of New Year on January first, according to the Gregorian Calendar, was instituted by Peter the Great in 1700. The previous evening is known as St. Sylvester's Eve, and is the time of great fun and enjoyment.

Ovsen, a mythological being peculiar to the season, is supposed to make his entry about this time, riding a boar (another indication of Aryan descent), and no Christmas or New Year's dinner is considered complete without pork served in some form. The name of Ovsen, being so like the French word for oats, suggests the possibility of this ancient god's supposed influence over the harvests, and the honor paid him at the ingathering feasts in Roman times. He is the god of fruitfulness, and on New Year's Eve Russian boys go from house to house scattering oats and other grain while they sing:

In the forest, in the pine forest,
There stood a pine tree,
Green and shaggy.
O Ovsen! O Ovsen!
The Boyars came,
Cut down the pine,
Sawed it into planks,
Built a bridge,
Covered it with cloth.

Fastened it with nails,
O Ovsen! O Ovsen!
Who, who will go
Along that bridge t
Ovsen will go there,
And the New Year,
O Ovsen! O Ovsen!

With this song the young folks endeavor to encourage the people who are about to cross the gulf between the known and the unknown, the Past and the Future Year; at the same time they scatter good seed for them to reap a bountiful harvest.

Often the boys sing the following Kolyadki:

Afield, afield, out in the open field!
There a golden plough goes ploughing,
And behind that plough is the Lord Himself. Holy Peter helps Him to drive,
And the Mother of God carries the seed corn,
Carries the seed corn, prays to the Lord God, Make, 0 Lord, the strong wheat to grow,
The strong wheat and the vigorous corn
The stalks there shall be like reeds!
The ears shall be (plentiful) as blades of
Grass!
The sheaves shall be (in number) like the stars
The stacks shall be like hills,
The loads shall be gathered together like
black clouds.

How singularly appropriate it seems that boys, hungry at all times, should be the ones to implore the god of fruitfulness to bestow upon their people an abundant harvest during the coming year!

In Petrograd the New Year is ushered in with a cannonade of one hundred shots fired at midnight. The Czar formally receives the good wishes of his subjects, and the streets, which are prettily decorated with flags and lanterns, are alive with people.

On New Year's Day the Winter Palace is opened to society, as is nearly every home in the city, for at this season, at least, hospitality and charity are freely dispensed from palace and cottage.

On Sotjelnik, the last of the holidays, the solemn service of Blessing the Water of the Neva is observed. At two o'clock in the afternoon the people who have gathered in crowds at various points along the river witness the ceremony which closes the festivities of Yule-tide. At Petrograd a dome is erected in front of the Winter Palace, where in the presence of a vast concourse of people the Czar and the high church officials in a grand and impressive manner perform the ceremony. In other places it is customary for the district priest to officiate. Clothed in vestments he leads a procession of clergy and villagers, who carry icons and banners and chant as they proceed to the river. They usually leave an open space in their ranks through which all the bad spirits likely to feel antagonistic to the ruler of Winter—the Frost King—may flee. For water sprites, fairies, gnomes, and other invisibilities, who delight in sunshine and warmth, are forced, through the power of the priest's prayers, and the showering of holy water, to take refuge in P, hole that is cut in the ice beside a tall cross, and disappear beneath the cold water of the blessed river.

Yule-tide in France

One would naturally assume that such a pleasure loving people as the French would make much of Christmas, but instead of this we find that with them, excepting in a few provinces and places remote from cities, it is the least observed of all the holidays.

It was once a very gay season, but now Paris scarcely recognizes the day excepting in churches. The shops, as in most large cities, display elegant goods, pretty toys, a great variety of sweetmeats, and tastefully trimmed Christmas trees, for that wonderful tree is fast spreading over Europe, especially wherever the Anglo-Saxon and Teutonic races have settled.

Confectioners offer a tempting supply of naulets—little delicate cakes—with a sugar figure of Christ on top, pretty boxes made of chocolate containing candy in the form of fruits, vegetables, musical instruments, and even boots and shoes, and all manner of quaint, artistic sugared devices, to be used as gifts or table decorations.

Early in December, wooden booths and open-air stands are erected throughout the shopping districts for the sale of Christmas goods. At night they are lighted, and through the day and evening they are gay with shoppers. Many of the booths contain evergreens and fresh green boughs for making the arbre de Nau. This is a hoop tied with bunches of green, interspersed with rosy apples, nuts, and highly colored, gaily ornamented egg shells that have been carefully blown for the purpose. The hoops are hung in sitting-rooms or kitchens, but are used more in the country than in the cities.

Although the cities are filled with Yule-tide shoppers and lovely wares, in order to enjoy a veritable Merry Christmas one must seek some retired town and if possible gain access to a home of ancient date, where the family keep the customs of their ancestors. There he will find the day devoutly and solemnly observed, and legend and superstitions concerning every observance of the day. He will find that great anxiety is evinced regarding the weather during the twelve days preceding Christmas, as that portends the state of the weather for the ensuing twelve months.

He will notice that unlike the Yule-logs of other countries, those of France are not to be sat on, for if by any chance a person sits on a Yule-log he will experience such pain as will prevent his partaking of the Christmas dinner. He will also find that the log has benevolent powers, and if his shoe is left beside it during the night it will be filled with peppermints or candy. The ashes of the log are believed to be a protection against lightning and bad luck, so some will be stored away beneath the bed of the master of the house as a means of procuring good-fortune and other blessings during the coming year, and if he chance to fall sick, some of the ashes will probably be infused into his medicine and given to him.

If the log, the cosse de Nau, is of oak and felled at midnight, it is supposed to be much more efficacious, therefore all who can do so procure an oaken log, at least. In some families where the Yule-log is lighted, it is the custom to have it brought into the room by the oldest and youngest members of the family. The oldest member is expected to pour three libations of wine upon the log while voicing an invocation in behalf of wealth, health, and general good-fortune for the household, after which the youngest member, be he a few days or a few months old, drinks to the newly lighted fire,—the emblem of the new light of another year. Each member present follows the example set by the youngest, and drinks to the new light.

Yule-tide in France begins on St. Barbar's Day, December fourth, when it is customary to plant grain in little dishes of earth for this saint's use as a means of informing her devotees what manner of crops to expect during the forthcoming year. If the grain comes up and is flourishing at Christmas, the crops will be abundant. Each dish of fresh, green grain is used for a centerpiece on the dinner table.

For several days previous to Christmas, children go into the woods and fields to gather laurel, holly, bright berries, and pretty lichens with which to build the cache, their tribute in commemoration of the birth of Christ. It is a representation of the Holy Manger, which the little folks build on a table in the corner of the living-room. With bits of stones they form a hill, partly covering the rocky surface with green and sometimes sprinkling it with flour to produce the effect of snow. On and about the hill they arrange tiny figures of men and beasts, and above the summit they suspend a bright star, a white dove, or a gilded figure of Jehovah.

After the ceremony of lighting the Yule-log on Christmas Eve, the children light up the crèche with small candles, often tri-colored in honor of the Trinity. Throughout the work of gathering the material and making and lighting the crèche, they sing carols in praise of the Little Jesus. In fact young and old accompany their Yule-tide labors with carols, such as their parents and grandparents sang before them,—the famous Noels of the country.

The children continue to light their crèche each night until Epiphany, the family gathering around and joining in singing one or more of the well-known Noels, for

Shepherds at the grange,
Where the Babe was born,
Sang, with many a change,
Christmas carols until morn.

Let us by the fire
Ever higher
Sing them till the night expires.

On the eve of Epiphany the children all march forth to meet the Magi, who are yearly expected, but who yearly disappoint the waiting ones.

The custom of hanging sheaves of wheat to the eaves of the houses for the birds' Christmas, so commonly observed throughout the cooler countries, is also observed by the children of France, and the animals are given especial care and attention at this joyous season. Each house cat is given all it can eat on Christmas Eve for if by any chance, it mews, bad luck is sure to follow. Of course a great deal is done for the poorer class at Christmas; food, clothing, and useful gifts are liberally bestowed, and so far as it is possible, the season is one of good will and good cheer for all.

If the French still hold to many of the Christmas customs bequeathed them by their Aryan ancestors, New Year's Day shows the influence of their Roman conquerors, for a combination of Northern and Southern customs is noticeable on that occasion. Each public official takes his seat of office on that day, after the manner of the Romans. Family feasting, exchanging of gifts among friends, and merrymaking are features of New Year's Day rather than of Christmas in France, although children delight in placing their sabots, or shoes, on the hearth for the Christ-child to fill with gifts on Christmas Eve.

In early times New Year's Day was the occasion of the Festival of Fools, when the wildest hilarity prevailed, and for upward of two hundred and forty years that custom continued in favor. Now Christmas is essentially the church festival; New Year's Day is the social festival, and Epiphany is the oldest festival observed during Yule-tide in France.

The latter festival is derived from the Roman Saturnalia, the main feature of the celebration being lawlessness and wild fun. Many of the features of former times are no longer in vogue, but the Twelfth-Night supper still continues in favor, when songs, toasts, and a general good time finishes the holiday season.

December is really the month of song in France. From the first to the last every one who can utter a sound is singing, singing, singing. Strolling musicians go from house to house playing and singing Noels, and old and young of all classes in society, at home and abroad, on their way to church or to market, at work or at play, may be heard singing these fascinating carols.

Noel signifies "good news," and it has been the greeting of the season since the earliest observance of Christmas. The word is on every tongue; salutations, invocations, and songs begin and end with it. Carols peculiarly adapted to the day or season in time came to be known as Noels, and these songs are to be heard everywhere in France during the holidays of Yule-tide.

Yule-tide in Italy

Italy! The land of Dante, Petrarch, Bocaccio, Raphael, Michelangelo, and a host of other shining lights in literature and art!

Can we imagine any one of them as a boy watching eagerly for Christmas to arrive; saving up money for weeks to purchase some coveted dainty of the season; rushing through crowded streets on Christmas Eve to view the Bambino, and possibly have an opportunity to kiss its pretty bare toe? How strange it all seems. Yet boys today probably do many of the same things they did in the long ago during the observance of this holy season in historic, artistic Italy.

In November, while flowers are yet in bloom, preparations are begun for the coming festivities. City streets and shops are crowded with Christmas shoppers, for beside all the gifts that are purchased by the Italians, there are those bought by travelers and foreign residents to be sent to loved ones at home, or to be used in their own observance of the day, which is usually after the manner of their respective countries. So shopping is lively from about the first of November until after the New Year.

The principal streets are full of carriages, the shops are full of the choicest wares, and it is to be hoped that the pocketbooks are full of money wherewith to purchase the beautiful articles displayed.

During the Novena, or eight days preceding Christmas, in some provinces shepherds go from house to house inquiring if Christmas is to be kept there. If it is, they leave a wooden spoon to mark the place, and later bring their bagpipes or other musical instruments and play before it, singing one of the sweet Nativity songs, of which the following is a favorite.

For ever hallow'd be
The night when Christ was born,
For then the saints did see
The holy star of morn.
So Anastasius and St. Joseph old
They did that blessed sight behold.

Chorus: (in which all present join)
When Father, Son and Holy Ghost unite
That man may saved be.

It is expected that those who have a presepio are ready by this time to receive guests to pray before it and strolling musicians to sing before it, for the presepio is the principal feature of an Italian Christmas. It is made as expensive as its owner can afford, and sometimes much more so. It is a miniature representation of the birthplace of Christ, showing the Holy Family—Joseph, Mary, and the infant Jesus in the manger—or, more frequently, the manger awaiting the infant. This is a doll that is brought in later, passed around that each person in the room may pray before it, and is then solemnly deposited in the manger. There are angels, and other figures several inches high, carved in wood—usually sycamore,—prettily colored and introduced to please the owner's taste; the whole is artistically arranged to represent the scene at Bethlehem which the season commemorates. When the festivities cease the presepio is taken apart and carefully stored away for use another year.

During the Novena, children go about reciting Christmas pieces, receiving money from those who gather around them to listen, and later they spend their earnings in buying eels or some other substantial delicacy of the season.

The Ceppo, or Yule-log, is lighted at two o'clock the day previous to Christmas, on the kitchen hearth in provinces where it is sufficiently cold to have a hearth, and fires are lighted in other rooms, for here as elsewhere fire and light are necessary adjuncts of Christmas. During the twenty-four hours preceding Christmas Eve a rigid fast is observed, and there is an absence of Christmas cheer in the atmosphere, for the season is strictly a religious one rather than of a social nature like that of Northern countries. At early twilight candles are lighted around the presepio, and the little folks recite before it some poem suitable for the occasion. Then follows the banquet made as elaborate as possible. The menu varies in different parts of the country, but in every part fish forms an important item of food. In many places a capon stuffed with chestnuts is considered indispensable, and the family purse is often stretched to its utmost to provide this luxury, yet rich and poor deem this one article of food absolutely necessary on this occasion. Macaroni is of course the ever-present dish on all occasions throughout the country, and various sweetmeats are abundantly provided.

Then comes the drawing of presents from the Urn of Fate; a custom common to many countries. As the parcels are interspersed with blanks, the drawing from the urn creates much excitement and no little disappointment among the children, who do not always understand that there will be a gift for each one notwithstanding the blanks.

There is no evergreen used in either church or home trimmings, but flowers, natural or artificial, are used instead. Soon after nine o'clock the people, young and old, leave their homes for some church in which the Christmas Eve services begin by ten o'clock.

Bright holly-berries, sweet violets, stately chrysanthemums, and pretty olive-trees bedecked with oranges,—such as are bought by those accustomed to having a Christmas tree,—are displayed in shops and along the streets, nearly all of which are hung with bright lanterns. The people carry flaming torches to add to the general brightness of the evening, and in some cities fireworks are set off. From their sun-worshiping Aryan ancestors Italy derives the custom of burning the ceppo, the love of light and fire, and many other customs. A few of these may be traced to Roman influence. Unfortunately many, very many, of the old customs, once so generally observed throughout Italy, are now passing out of use.

During the past few years several benevolent societies have distributed presents among the poor and needy at Christmas time, an event that is known as the Albero di Natale—The Tree of Nativity,—but little boys and girls of Italy do not yet know the delight of having a real Christmas tree hung with lovely gifts, such as we have in America.

At sunset on Christmas Eve the booming of cannon from the Castle of St. Angelo announces the beginning of the Holy Season. Papal banners are displayed from the castle, and crowds wend their way toward St. Peter's, the object of every one's desire who is so fortunate as to be in Rome at this season, for there the service is the most magnificent in the world. Every Roman Catholic Church is crowded on Holy Night with men, women, and children, anxious to see the procession of church officials in their beautiful robes, who carry the Bambino about the church for the worshipers to behold and kiss its robes or its toe. The larger the church the more beautiful the sight generally, although to a Protestant beholder the smaller churches with their enforced simplicity often prove more satisfactory to the spirit of worship.

But whether the officials are clothed in scarlet robes, ermine capes, and purple cassocks, and the walls covered with silken hangings of gold and crimson, with thousands of wax tapers lighted, and real flowers adorning the altar and organ pipes; whether the Madonna on the left of the altar is attired in satin and gleaming with precious jewels, and the presepio on the right is a marvel of elegance, with the Bambino wrapped in gold and silver tissue studded with jewels; or whether all is of an humble, simple character; the devout watch eagerly for the appearance of the Babe to be laid in the manger when the midnight bells peal forth the glad tidings of its birth. In each church the organ sounds its joyous accompaniment to the sweet voices of the choir which sings the Magnificat. The music is in itself a rare treat to listeners as it is always the best, the very best that can be procured. At two o'clock on Christmas morning the Shepherds' Hymn is chanted, and at five o'clock the first High Mass is held. In some of the larger churches solemn vespers are held Christmas afternoon, when the Holy Cradle is carried around among the audience.

At St. Peter's it is required that all the men present shall wear dress-suits and that the women be clothed in black, which offsets the brilliancy of the robes worn by the church officials, for even the guards on duty are in elegant red and white uniforms. About ten o'clock in the evening a procession of monks, priests, bishops, and cardinals, walking two and two, enters the vast building just as the great choir of male voices with organ accompaniment sounds forth the Magnificat. The procession is long, glowing in color, and very attractive to the eye, but the object of each Romanist's desire is to see the Pope, who, in magnificent robes, and seated in his crimson chair, is borne aloft on the shoulders of four men clothed in violet. On the Pope's head gleams his richly gemmed tiara and his heavy robes sparkle with costly jewels. Waving in front of His Eminence are two huge fans of white ostrich feathers set with eyes of peacock feathers, to signify the purity and watchfulness of this highest of church functionaries. Before His Holiness march the sixty Roman noblemen, his Guard of Honor, who form his escort at all church festivals, while Cardinals, Bishops, and others, according to their rank, march beside him, or near at hand.

With his thumb and two fingers extended in recognition of the Trinity, and at the same time showing the ring of St. Peter which he always wears, the Pope, followed by the ecclesiastic procession, passes down the nave between the files of soldiers, blessing the people as he goes.

Upon reaching the altar the Pope is escorted to an elevated seat while the choir sings the Psalm of Entrance. Later, at the elevation of the Host, the cannon of St. Angelo (the citadel of Rome, which was built in the time of the Emperor Hadrian) booms forth and every Roman Catholic bows his head in prayer, where so ever he may be. At the close of the service the gorgeous procession is again formed and the Pope is carried out of the church, blessing the multitude as he passes.

New Year is the great Social feature of Yule-tide in Italy. Visits and some presents are exchanged among friends, dinner parties, receptions, and fetes of all kinds are in order, but all interest centers in the church observances until Epiphany, or Bafana, as Italians term it, when children hang up their stockings, ceppo boxes are exchanged, and people indulge in home pleasures to some extent. The wild hilarity of the Saturnalian festivities of former times is fast dying out, for the growth of cities and towns has not proved conducive to such observances, and only in the smaller places is anything of the sort observed.

Yule-tide in Italy at the present day is principally a church festival.

Yule-tide in Spain

In Spain, the land of romance and song, of frost and flowers, where at Yule-tide the mountains wear a mantle of pure white snow while flowers bloom gaily in field and garden, the season's observance approaches more nearly than in any other country to the old Roman Saturnalia.

The Celts who taught the Spaniards the love of ballads and song left some traces of the sun-worshipers' traditions, but they are few in comparison with those of other European countries. Spain is a land apparently out of the line of Wodin's travel and influence, where one looks in vain for the mysterious mistletoe, the pretty holly, and the joyful Christmas tree.

The season is rigidly observed in churches, but otherwise it loses its spirit of devotion in that of wild revelry. Music, mirth, and hilarity are the leading features of the occasion, and home and family pleasures are secondary affairs.

Of course the customs vary in different provinces, some of which still cling to primitive forms of observance while others are fast adopting those of foreign residents and becoming Continental in style. But everywhere throughout the land Christmas is the day of days,—the great church festival observed by all.

The Noche-buena or Good Night, preceding Christmas, finds the shops gay with sweets and fancy goods suitable for holiday wear, but not with the pretty gifts such as circulate from home to home in northern countries, for here gifts are not generally exchanged.

Doctors, ministers, and landlords receive their yearly gifts of turkeys, cakes, and produce from their dependents, but the love of presenting dainty Christmas gifts has not reached the land of the three C's—the Cid, Cervantes, and Columbus.

Do you know what you would probably do if you were a dark-cheeked Spanish lad named Miguel, or a bright-eyed, light-hearted Spanish maiden named Dolores?

If you were Miguel you would don your black jacket and brown trousers, knot your gayest kerchief around your neck, and with your guitar in hand you would hasten forth to enjoy the fun that prevails in every street of every town in Spain on Christmas Eve, or, as it is known there, the Noche-buena.

If you were pretty Dolores you would surely wear your red or yellow skirt, or else of striped red and yellow, your best embroidered velvet jacket,—handed down from mother to daughter, and a wonderful sample of the handiwork that once made the country famous,—your numerous necklaces and other ornaments. You would carefully braid your heavy dark tresses and bedeck your shapely head with bright flowers, then with your panderetta or tambourine in hand, you too would join the merry throng that fill the air with mirthful songs and music on Noche-buena; for remember,

This is the eve of Christmas,
No sleep from now till morn.

The air is full of the spirit of unrest, castanets click joyously, tambourines jingle their silvery strains, while guitars and other musical instruments help to swell the babel of sound preceding the hour of the midnight mass:

At twelve will the child be born,

and if you have not already done some especially good deed to some fellow mortal, you will hasten to clear your conscience by such an act before the bells announce the hour of its birth. As the stars appear in the heavens, tiny oil lamps are lighted in every house, and among all devout Roman Catholics the image of the Virgin is illuminated with a taper.

The streets, which in many cities are brilliantly lighted with electricity, are crowded with turkeys awaiting purchasers. They are great fat birds that have been brought in from the country and together with quacking ducks and cooing pigeons help to swell the sounds that fill the clear, balmy air. Streets and market-places are crowded with livestock, while every other available spot is piled high with delicious fruit;—golden oranges, sober-hued dates, and indispensable olives; and scattered among these are cheeses of all shapes and kinds, sweetmeats of all sorts, the choice candies that are brought from various provinces, and quaint pigskins of wine. No wonder every one who can do so hurries forth into the street on Noche-buena.

If you are not tempted to stop and gaze at these appetizing exhibits, you will pass quickly on to the brightly lighted booths devoted to toys. Oh, what a feast for young eyes. Here yours will surely light on some coveted treasure. It may be an ordinary toy, a drum, a horn, or it may be a Holy Manger, Shepherds, The Wise Men, or even a Star of the East.

It is hard to keep one's purse closed among such a surfeit of tempting articles, and everywhere money flows freely from hand to hand, although the Spanish are usually very frugal.

As the bells clang out the hour of midnight, you will hurry to join the throng wending its way to the nearest church, where priests in their gorgeous robes,—some of them worn only on this occasion and precious with rare embroidery and valuable jewels,—perform the midnight or cock-crow mass, and where the choir and the priests chant a sweet Christmas hymn together. What if it is late when the service ends? Christmas Eve without dancing is not to be thought of in Spain. So you go forth to find a group of Gipsy dancers who are always on hand to participate in this great festival; or you watch the graceful Spanish maiden in her fluffy skirts of lace, with her deep pointed bodice, a bright flower in her coal-black hair beside the tall comb, and her exquisitely shaped arms adorned with heavy bracelets. "Oh, what magnificent eyes. What exquisite long lashes!" you exclaim to yourself. See her poise an instant with the grace of a sylph, one slippered foot just touching the floor, then click, click, sound the castanets, as they have sounded for upwards of two thousand years and are likely to do for two thousand more, for their inspiriting click seems necessary to move Spanish feet and give grace to the uplifted arms. At first she may favor you with the energetic fandango, or the butterfly-like bolero, but on Christmas Eve the Jota is the universal favorite. It is danced and sung to music which has been brought down to the present time unwritten, and which was passed from mouth to mouth through many generations. Translated the words read:

Of Jesus the Nativity is celebrated everywhere,
Everywhere reigns contentment, everywhere reigns pleasure,

the audience joining in the refrain:

Long live merrymaking, for this is a day of rejoicing,
And may the perfume of pleasure sweeten our existence.

It will probably be late into the morning before the singing, dancing, thoughtless crowd turns homeward to rest, and although it is certainly a crowd intoxicated with pleasure, it is never in that condition from liquor.

There are three masses on Christmas Day, and all devout Catholics attend one of them at least, if not all. In some places Nativity plays are given on Christmas Eve or else on Christmas Day. They are long performances, but never tedious to the audiences, because the scenes appeal to them with the force of absolute realism. On Christmas morning the postmen, telegraph boys, and employees of various vocations, present to their employers and others little leaflets containing a verse appropriate to the day, or the single sentence "A Happy Christmas," expecting to receive in return a Christmas box filled with goodies of some kind.

While Spanish children do not have the Christmas tree to gather around they do have the pretty Nacimiento, made of plaster and representing the place of Christ's nativity, with the manger, tiny men and women, trees, and animals, such as are supposed to have existed at the time and place of the Nativity.

The Nacimiento (meaning being born) is lighted with candles, and little folks dance gaily around it to the music of tambourines and their own sweet voices, joyously singing one of the pretty Nativity songs. Groups of children go about the streets singing these songs of which there are many.

In this pleasing custom of the Nacimiento one sees a vestige of the Saturnalia, for during that festival small earthenware figures used to be for sale for the pleasure of children. Although the Spanish race is a mixed one and various peoples have been in power from time to time, at one period the country was, with the exception of Basque, entirely Romanized. It is interesting to note the lingering influence of this mighty Roman nation and find in this century that some of the main features of the great Roman feast are retained in the great Christian feast at Yuletide.

Southern races were always firm believers in Fate. The Mohammedans reverenced the Tree of Fate, but the Romans held sacred the urn containing the messages of Fate. So the Spaniards cling to the urn, from which at Christmas gatherings of friends it is the custom to draw the names of the men and women whom Fate ordains shall be devoted friends during the year,—the men performing all the duties of lovers. This drawing of one's Fate for the coming year creates great merriment and often no little disappointment. But Fate is inexorable and what is to be must be, so the Spanish maiden accepts graciously the one Fate thus assigns her.

After the midday breakfast on Christmas morning the people usually seek out-of-door pleasures. Among many of the old families only blood relations are expected to eat and drink together on this holy day.

Ordinarily the Spaniard "may find perfect entertainment in a crust of bread and a bit of garlic" as the proverb claims, but at Yule-tide his stomach demands many delicacies peculiar to the season. The Puchero Olla, the national dish for dinner, must have a few extra ingredients added on this occasion. The usual compound of chickens, capons, bacon, mutton, beef, pig's feet, lard, garlic, and everything else the larder affords, is quite insufficient to be boiled together on this occasion. However, if one has no relatives to invite him to a feast, it is an easy matter to secure a Christmas dinner on the streets, where men are ready to cook for him over their braseros of charcoal and venders are near at hand to offer preserved fruits, the famous almond rock, almond soup, truffled turkey, or the most desirable of the season's delicacies,—sea-bream, which is brought from Cadiz especially for Christmas use, and which is eaten at Christmas in accordance with the old-time custom. Nuts of all kinds are abundant. By the side of the streets, venders of chestnuts—the finest in the world—lean against their clumsy two-wheeled carts, picturesque in costumes that are ragged and soiled from- long service. Rich layer-cakes of preserves, having almond icing with fruits and liquor-filled ornaments of sugar on top, are frequently sent from friend to friend for dinner.

In Seville, and possibly in other places, the people hurry to the cathedral early in the afternoon in order to secure good places before the high altar from which to view the Siexes, or dances. Yes, dances! This ceremony takes place about five o'clock just as the daylight fades and night draws near. Ten choristers and dancers, indiscriminately termed Siexes, appear before the altar clad in the costume of Seventeenth-Century pages, and reverently and with great earnestness sing and dance an old-time minuet, with castanet accompaniment, of course. The opening song is in honor of the Virgin, beginning:

Hail, 0 Virgin, most pure and beautiful.

Among the ancients dancing was a part of religious services, but it is now seldom seen in churches. This Christmas dance, given in a beautiful cathedral just at the close of day, is a very impressive ceremony and forms a fitting close to the Spanish Christmas, which is so largely made up of customs peculiar to ancient and modern races.

In every part of Spain song and dance form an important part of the festivities of Yule-tide, which lasts two weeks, although the laboring class observe but two days of pleasure. At the palace the King holds a reception on New Year's, not for the public generally, but for the diplomats and grandees.

The higher circles of society observe New Year as a time of exchanging calls and visiting, feasting and merrymaking. At the banquets of the wealthy every possible delicacy in the way of food is temptingly displayed, and great elegance in dress indulged in by the ladies, who wear their finest gowns and adorn themselves in priceless jewels and rare laces. But there is so much etiquette to be observed among this class of Spaniards that one looks for the real enjoyment of the season among the common classes.

In some parts of Spain bull-fights are given as late as December, but cold weather has a softening effect on the poor bulls and makes them less ferocious, so unless the season proves unusually warm that favorite entertainment has to be abandoned for a time. Meanwhile in the streets and homes one may often see a father on all fours enacting the infuriated bull for his little sons to attack; in this way he teaches them the envied art of bull-fighting. The Yule-tide festivities end at Twelfth Day,—Epiphany, when crowds of young folks go from gate to gate in the cities to meet the Magi, and after much merriment they come to the conclusion that the Magi will not appear until the following year.

Yule-tide in America

To people who go into a new country to live, Christmas, which is so generally a family day, must of necessity be a lonely, homesick one. They carry with them the memory of happy customs, of loved ones far away, and of observances which can never be held again. So many of the earliest Christmases in America were peculiarly sad ones to the various groups of settlers; most especially was this the case with the first Christmas ever spent by Europeans in the New World.

The intrepid mariner, Christopher Columbus, entered the port of Bohio, in the Island of Haiti, on St. Nicholas Day, December 6, 1492, and in honor of the day named that port Saint Nicholas. The Pinta with her crew had parted from the others and gone her own way, so the Santa Maria and the Nina sailed on together, occasionally stopping where the port seemed inviting. While in one of these, Columbus heard of rich mines not far distant and started for them. The Admiral and his men were tired from continued watching, and as the sea was smooth and the wind favorable, they went to sleep leaving the ship in care of a boy. Who he was no one knows, but he was evidently the first Christian boy to pass a Christmas Eve on this continent,—and a sad one it was for him. The ship struck a sand-bank and settled, a complete wreck, in the waters of the New World. Fortunately no lives were lost, and the wreckage furnished material for the building of a fortress which occupied the men's time during the remainder of the Yule-tide.

The Nina was too small to accommodate two crews, therefore on Christmas Day many of the men were wondering who were to stay on that faraway island among the strange looking natives of whom they knew nothing.

The Chief of Guarico (Petit Anse), whom Columbus was on his way to visit at the time of the disaster, sent a fleet of canoes to the assistance of the strangers, and did what he could to make them happy during the day. The Spaniards and the natives worked until dawn on Christmas morning, bringing ashore what they could secure from the wreck, and storing it away on the island for future use. Strange to relate, they succeeded in saving all of their provisions, the spars, and even many of the nails of the wrecked Santa Maria. But what a Christmas morning for Columbus and his men, stranded on an island far, far from home, among a strange people. There were no festivities to be observed by that sad, care-worn company of three hundred men on that day, but the following morning Chief Guacanagari visited the Nina and took Columbus ashore, where a banquet was prepared in his honor, the first public function attended by Columbus in America. It can be pictured only in imagination. There on that beautiful island which seemed to them a paradise on earth, with tall trees waving their long fronds in the warm breeze, with myriads of birds such as they had never seen filling the air with song, Columbus stood, attired in his gorgeous uniform and dignified, as it befitted him to be, beside his host who was elegantly dressed in a shirt and a pair of gloves which Columbus had given him, with a coronet of gold on his head. The visiting chieftains with gold coronets moved about in nature's garb, among the "thousand,"—more or less,—who were present as guests. The feast consisted of shrimps, cassavi, —the same as the native bread of to-day,—and some of their nutritive roots.

It was not a sumptuous repast although it may have been a bountiful one, yet they probably enjoyed it.

The work of building a fortress began at once. Within ten days the Fortress of Navidad was completed. It stood on a hill and was surrounded with a broad, deep ditch for protection against natives and animals, and was to be the home of those of the company who remained in the New World, for the Nina was too small to convey all hands across the ocean to Spain, and nothing had been heard of the Pinta. Leaving biscuits sufficient for a year's supply, wine, and such provisions as could be spared, Columbus bade farewell to the forty men whom he was never to see again, and sailed for the Old World on January 4, 1493.

So far as recorded, Columbus was the only one among the Spaniards who received gifts during this first Yule-tide in America. But what seemed a cruel fate to him was the means of bestowing a valuable gift upon the world. Had the Santa Maria continued her course in safety that Christmas Eve there might never have been a fortress or any European settlement founded. So, although it was a sad, troubled Yule-tide to the Spanish adventurers, it proved a memorable one in the annals of America.

Four hundred years later the anchor of the Santa Maria was discovered and brought to the United States to be one of its treasured exhibits at the great Columbian Exposition, where a descendant of Columbus was the honored guest of the Government.

One hundred and fifty years after the building of the Fortress of Navidad, after many ineffectual attempts, a settlement was effected in the New World by a colony from England. They sailed from Blackwell, on the Thames, on December 19, 1606, and for six weeks were "knocking about in sight of England." Their first Christmas was spent within sight of their old homes. According to Captain John Smith's account, "It was, indeed but a sorry Christmas that we spent on board," as many of them were very sick, yet Smith adds, "We made the best cheer we could." The colonists landed, and solemnly founded Jamestown on May 13, 1607. That year Yule-tide was spent by Captain Smith among the Powhatan Indians, by whom he was taken captive. This colony consisted of men only; no genuine Christmas observance could take place without women and children, and no women arrived until 1609, and then only twenty came. But after the ninety young women arrived in 1619, supplied to planters for one hundred pounds of tobacco each, and a cargo of twenty Negros had landed to help with the work, there may have been an attempt at keeping Christmas although there is no record of the fact.

At this season there was usually a raid made upon the Indians. Smith's last expedition against them was at Christmastime, when, as he records in his journal, "The extreme wind, rain, frost, and snow caused us to keep Christmas among the salvages where we were never more merry, nor fed on more plenty of good Oysters, Fish, Flesh, Wild Fowl and good bread, nor never had better fires in England."

In after years prosperity smiled on the land of the Jamestown settlers. Amidst the peace and plenty that followed the earlier years of strife and poverty, the Virginians became noted for their hospitality and lavish observance of Yule-tide. It was the happy home-coming for daughters, sons, uncles, aunts, and cousins of the first, second, and even the third degree. For whosoever was of the name and lineage, whether rich or poor, was welcomed at this annual ingathering of the family. Every house was filled to overflowing; great hickory fires were lighted on the open hearths; the rooms were brilliantly lighted with candles, and profusely trimmed with greens. From doors and ceilings were hung sprigs of the mysterious mistletoe, for

O'er the lover
I'll shake the berry'd mistletoe; that
he May long remember Christmas,

was the thought of merry maidens as they decorated their homes.

Christmas brought carriage-loads of guests to these old-time homes, to partake of the good cheer and enjoy weeks of fun and frolic, indoors and out. For many days before Christmas arrived, colored cooks, the regular, and extra ones, were busy cooking from morning till evening, preparing for the occasion. The storerooms were replete with every variety of tempting food the ingenious minds of the cooks could devise, for Christmas dinner was the one great test of their ability and woe to Auntie whose fire was too hot, or whose judgment was at fault on this occasion.

To the whites and blacks Christmas was a season of peace, plenty, and merriment. In the "Great House" and in the cabin there were music, dancing, and games until New Year. This was "Hiring Day," and among the blacks joy was turned to sadness as husbands, fathers, brothers, and lovers were taken away to work on distant plantations, for those who hired extra help through the year were often extremely cruel in their treatment of the slaves.

The gladsome Virginia Christmas in time became the typical one of the South, where it was the red-letter day of the year, the most joyous of all holidays. The churches were lovingly and tastefully decorated with boughs of green and flowers by the ladies themselves and conscientiously attended by both old and young. In the South there was never any of the somberness that attended church services in the North among descendants of the Plymouth Colony who came to America later.

The Puritans of England early discountenanced the observance of Christmas. But among the Pilgrims who reached the American coast in December, 1620, were mothers who had lived so long in Holland they loved the old-time custom of making merry on that day. To these dear women, and to the kind-hearted, child-loving Elder Brewster, we are indebted for the first observance of the day held by the Plymouth Colony.

According to the Journal of William Bradford, kept for so many years, the Pilgrims went ashore, "and ye 25 day (Dec.) begane to erecte ye first house for comone use to receive them and their goods." Bradford conscientiously refrains from alluding to the day as Christmas, but descendants of these godly Puritans are glad to learn that homemaking in New England was begun on Christmas Day.

Many very interesting stories have been written about this first Christmas. One writer even pictures the more lenient Elder Brewster as going ashore that morning and inviting the Indian Chief Massasoit to go aboard the Mayflower with him. According to the story, the good man endeavored to impress the chief with the solemnity and significance of the occasion, and then with Massasoit, two squaws, and six boys and girls, becomingly attired in paint and feathers, he returned to the ship.

The women and children from over the sea met their new neighbors and guests, received from them little baskets of nuts and wintergreen berries, and in exchange gave their guests beads, toys, raisins, and such simple gifts, to which Elder Brewster added a blessing bestowed upon each child.

The story reads well. But the truth, according to history, makes the first visit of Massasoit occur some three months later, on March twenty-second. The Puritans had a happy Christmas dinner together on board the ship which was the only home they possessed as yet, and it is to be presumed that the exceedingly conscientious non-observers of the day partook quite as freely of the salt fish, bacon, Brussels sprouts, gooseberry tarts, and English plum pudding, as did those homesick, tear-choked women who prepared the dinner.

It is certainly to be regretted that vessels are no longer built with the wonderful storage capacity of the Mayflower. Beside bringing over the innumerable family relics that are treasured throughout this country, it is stated that this ship brought a barrel full of ivy, holly, laurel, and immortelles, with which the table was decorated, and wreaths woven for the children to wear. Bless those dear, brave women who dared to bring "green stuff" for "heathenish decorations" way across the ocean. Let us add a few extra sprays of green each Christmas in memory of them. The greens, plum puddings, and other good things had such a happy affect that, according to Bradford, "at night the master caused us to have some Beere." This was an event worthy of a capital B, as the men had worked all day in the biting cold at house-building, with only a scanty supply of water to drink.

Alas! That Christmas on the Mayflower was the last the Pilgrims were to enjoy for many a long year. Other ship-loads of people arrived during the year and in 1621, "One ye day called Christmas Day, ye Gov. called them out to work (as was used), but ye most of this new company excused themselves and said it went against their consciences to work on that day. So ye Gov. told them that if they made it matter of conscience, he would spare them till they were better informed. So he led away ye rest and left them, but when they came home at noon from their work, he found them in ye streets at play, openly, some pitching ye bair, and some at stools-ball, and such like sports. So he went to them and took away their implements, and told them that it was against his conscience, that they should play and others work. If they made ye keeping of it mater of devotion, let them keep their houses, but there should be no gaming or reveling in ye streets. Since which time nothing had been attempted that way, at least openly." And thus ended the last attempt at Christmas observance during Governor Bradford's many terms of office.

The Massachusetts Colony that arrived in 1630, and settled in and around Boston, believed that Christ's mission on earth as the Savior of man was too serious a one to be celebrated by the fallen race He came to save; they considered it absolutely wicked for anyone to be lively and joyous when he could not know whether or not he was doomed to everlasting punishment. Besides that, jollity often led to serious results. Were not the jails of Old England full to repletion the day after Christmas? It was wisest, they thought, to let the day pass unnoticed. And so only occasionally did any one venture to remember the fact of its occurrence. Among the men and women who came across the ocean during succeeding years there must have been many who differed from the first colony in regard to Christmas, for in May, 1659, the General Court of Massachusetts deemed it necessary to enact a law: "That whosoever shall be found observing any such day as Christmas or the like, either by forbearing of labor, feasting, or any other way, upon any such accounts as aforesaid, shall be subjected to a fine of five shillings."

For upward of twenty-two years it remained unlawful in Massachusetts to have a merry Christmas. There were no pretty gifts on that day to make happy little God-be-thanked, Search-the-scriptures, Seek-wisdom, Prudence, Hope, or Charity. However, Santa Claus had emissaries abroad in the land. In December, 1686, Governor Andros, an Episcopalian, and a representative of the King, brought about the first concession in favor of the day. He believed in celebrating Christmas and intended to hold appropriate services. The law enacted by Parliament in June, 1647, abolishing the observance of the day, had been repealed in 1659, and Gov. Andros knew he had the law in his favor. But every meetinghouse was conscientiously (or stubbornly) closed to him. So he was forced to hold service in the Town House, going with an armed soldier on each side to protect him from the "good will" exhibited by his fellow townsmen. He held services that day, and it is believed to be the first observance of Christmas held under legal sanction in Boston.

The great concession was made by the Old South Congregation in 1753 when it offered its sanctuary to the worshipers in King's Chapel, after that edifice was burned, for them to hold their Christmas services. It was with the implicit understanding that there was to be no spruce, holly, or other greens used on that occasion to desecrate their meeting-house.

Little by little the day was brought into favor as a holiday, but it was as late as the year 1856, while Nathaniel P. Banks was Governor, that the day was made a legal holiday in Massachusetts.

The good Dutch Fathers, true to the teachings of their forefathers, sailed for the New World with the image of St. Nicholas for a figurehead on their vessel. They named the first church they built for the much-loved St. Nicholas and made him patron saint of the new city on Manhattan Island. Thanks, many many thanks, to these sturdy old Dutchmen with unpronounceable names who preserved to posterity so many delightful customs of Christmas observance. What should we have done without them?

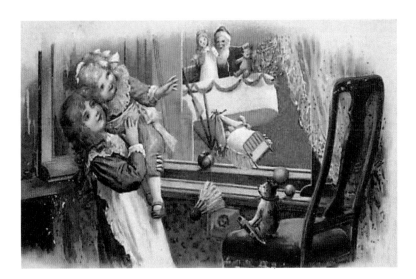

They were quite a worthy people notwithstanding they believed in enjoying life and meeting together for gossip and merrymaking. Christmas was a joyful season with them. The churches and quaint gabled houses were trimmed with evergreens, great preparations were made for the family feasts, and business was generally suspended. The jolly old City Fathers took a prolonged rest from cares of office, even ordering on December 14, 1654, that, " As the winter and the holidays are at hand, there shall be no more ordinary meetings of this board (the City Corporation) between this date and three weeks after Christmas. The Court messenger is ordered not to summon anyone in the meantime."

Sensible old souls. They were not going to allow business to usurp their time and thought during this joyful season.

The children must have their trees, hung with gifts; the needy must be especially cared for, and visits must be exchanged; so the City was left to take care of itself, while each household was busy making ready for the day of days, the season of seasons.

What a time those hausfraus had polishing up their silver, pewter, brass, and copper treasures, in opening up best rooms, and newly sanding the floors in devious intricate designs. What a pile of wood was burned to bake the huge turkeys, pies, and puddings. What pains the fathers took to select the rosiest apples and the choicest nuts to put in each child's stocking on Christmas Eve. Fortunately, children obeyed the injunction of Scripture in those days, and despised not the day of small things.

How fortunate it was that there were no trains or other rapid modes of conveyance to bring visitors from the Puritan Colonies at this season. There was no possibility of any of their strict neighbors dropping in unexpectedly to furnish a free lecture, while the Dutch families were merrily dancing. The Puritans were located less than two hundred and eighty-five miles distant, yet they were more distantly separated by ideas than by space. But a little leaven was eventually to penetrate the entire country, and the customs that are now observed each Christmas throughout the Eastern, Middle, and Western States, are mainly such as were brought to this' country by the Dutch. Americans have none of their own. In fact, they possess but little that is distinctively their own because they are a conglomerate nation, speaking a conglomerate language.

According to the late Lawrence Hutton, "Our Christmas carols appear to have come from the Holy Land itself; our Christmas trees from the East by way of Germany; our Santa Claus from Holland; our stockings hung in the chimney, from France or Belgium; and our Christmas cards and verbal Christmas greetings, our Yule logs, our boars' heads, our plum puddings and our mince pies from England. Our turkey is, seemingly, our only contribution." Let us add the squash-pie.

These customs which have become general throughout the United States, varying of course in different localities, are being rapidly introduced into the new possessions where they are engrafted on some of the prettiest customs observed by the people in former years. In Porto Rico on Christmas Day church procession of children in beautiful costumes, which is a very attractive feature. The people feast, dance, attend midnight mass on Christmas Eve, then dance and feast until Christmas morning. In fact they dance and feast most of the time from December twenty-fourth until January seventh, when not at church services. On Twelfth Night gifts are exchanged, for as yet Santa Claus has not ventured to visit such a warm climate, so the children continue to receive their gifts from the Holy Kings. However, under the shelter of the American Flag, the Christmas tree is growing in favor. In Hawaii, so far as possible, the so-called New England customs prevail.

In the Philippines even beggars in the streets expect a "Christmas present," which they solicit in good English.

So from Alaska to the Island of Tutuila, the smallest of America's possessions, Yule-tide is observed in a similar manner.

Yule-tide has been singularly connected with important events in the history of the United States.

In the year 1776 Washington crossed the Delaware on Christmas night to capture nearly one thousand Hessians after their Christmas revelries. A few days later, December 30th, Congress resolved to send Commissioners to the courts of Vienna, Spain, France, and Tuscany; and as victory followed the American leader, the achievements of this Yule-tide were declared by Frederick the Great of Prussia to be "the most brilliant of any recorded in the annals of military action." The year following, 1777, was probably one of the gloomiest Yule-tides in the experience of the American forces. They lay encamped at Valley Forge, sick and discouraged, destitute of food, clothing, and most of the necessities of life.

It was on Christmas Eve, 1783, that Washington laid aside forever his military clothes and assumed those of a civilian, feeling, as he expressed it, "relieved of a load of public care." After Congress removed to Philadelphia, Martha Washington held her first public reception in the Executive Mansion on Christmas Eve, when, it is stated, there was gathered "the most brilliant assemblage ever seen in America."

At Yule-tide a few years later, 1799, the country was mourning the death of the beloved Father of his Country.

In later years, the season continued prominent in the history of great events. The most notable of these were the two Proclamations of President Lincoln, the one freeing the slaves, January 1, 1863, and the other proclaiming the "unconditional pardon and amnesty to all concerned in the late insurrection," on December 25, 1868. And may the peace then declared remain with this people forevermore.

The end.

8147861R00039

Printed in Great Britain
by Amazon.co.uk, Ltd.,
Marston Gate.